WHAT IS A BIRD?

Robert Snedden

Photographs by Oxford Scientific Films

Illustrated by Adrian Lascom

Sierra Club Books for Children
San Francisco

For Zara

The Sierra Club, founded in 1892 by John Muir, has devoted itself to the study and protection of the earth's scenic and ecological resources — mountains, wetlands, woodlands, wild shores and rivers, deserts and plains. The publishing program of the Sierra Club offers books to the public as a nonprofit educational service in the hope that they may enlarge the public's understanding of the Club's basic concerns. The Sierra Club has some sixty chapters in the United States and in Canada. For information about how you may participate in its programs to preserve wilderness and the quality of life, please address inquiries to Sierra Club, 85 Second Street, San Francisco, CA 94105.

First Paperback Edition 1997

First published in Great Britain in 1992 by
Belitha Press Limited,
a member of Chrysalis Books Plc.
64 Brewery Road, London N7 9NT

Library of Congress Cataloging-in-Publication Data

Snedden, Robert.
    What is a bird?/Robert Snedden;
photographs by Oxford Scientific Films; illustrated
by Adrian Lascom. — 1st U.S. ed.
      p. cm.
    Includes index
    Summary: Describes the physical
characteristics of birds, how they fly, lay eggs,
and differ from other animals.
    ISBN 0-87156-539-0 (hc)
    ISBN 0-87156-922-1 (pb)
    1. Birds—Juvenile literature. [1. Birds.]
I. Lascom, Adrian, ill. II. Oxford Scientific Films.
III. Title.
QL676.2.S615
598—dc20   92-35059

Printed in Hong Kong
10 9 8 7 6 5 4 3 2

Editor: Rachel Cooke
Designer: Frances McKay
Picture researcher: Susan Mennell
Consultant: Dr. Jim Flegg
Educational consultant: Brenda Hart

The publisher wishes to thank the following for permission to reproduce copyrighted material:

Oxford Scientific Films and individual copyright holders on the following pages: Doug Allan, 4, 7; Ra Ben-Shahar, 5; Raymond Blythe, 24; Roger Brown, 23; Martyn Chillmaid, 9; John Downer, 28/29; Michael Fogden, 19; Bob Fredrick, 7; Arthur Gloor/Animals Animals, 19; Philippe Henry, 14; Michael Leach, 15; Roland Mayr, 22, 23; Patti Murray/Animals Animals, 4; Alan G. Nelson/Animals Animals 1; Ben Osborne, 9, 17; Stan Osolinski, cover, 3, 6/ 8, 25; Richard Packwood, 24, 27; Peter Parks, 24; C. M. Perrins, 27; Hans Reinhard/Okapia, 10, 16; Leonard Lee Rue III/Animals Animals, 11; Alastair Shay, 5; Tony Tilford, 11, 12/13.

Front cover picture
Lilac-breasted rolle

Title page picture:
A hummingbird
hovers in front of a
flower to feed on the
sugary nectar insid

Contents page pict
This is a saddleba
stork, which come
from Africa.

CONTENTS

WHAT IS A BIRD?

What is it that you think of when you think of a bird? How can so many different things – from ostriches to flamingoes and parrots to penguins – all be birds? Is a bird something that has feathers and flies? Is it something that has a beak and sings? Is it something that lays eggs?

Penguins live mainly around the icy shores of the Antarctic. They cannot fly, but their wings make excellent paddles for swimming. ▼

Flamingoes have huge beaks. They use these to strain the tiny plants and animals they eat from the water. ▶

Birds aren't the only animals that fly or sing. Bats can fly and people can sing. And they aren't the only animals that lay eggs. Flies, frogs and fish all do, for example.

So what is it that makes a bird a bird? What exactly is a bird?

This book will show you something of the way the living creatures we call birds work. You'll see some of the things they have in common with other animals and find out what it is that makes them different.

The ostrich is the largest bird in the world. It cannot fly, but it runs very fast!

Parrots are colorful birds. They can often be heard screeching noisily in the jungles and forests where they live.

FEATHERS

Every bird has feathers. Feathers are what make birds different from everything else because no other animal has them. If an animal has feathers, then it is a bird.

Feathers are light, strong and flexible. They are made from a tough substance called **keratin**. This is the same thing that your hair and nails and the scales of a reptile are made of. A bird's feathers keep it warm and dry and also help to protect its body from injury. And, of course, without its feathers no bird could fly!

All of the feathers of a bird together are called its **plumage**. There are two main types of feather. These are **contour feathers** and **down feathers**.

The contour feathers are the ones that give the bird its shape and its markings. A bird's wings and tail are made up of specially shaped contour feathers. Contour feathers look flat and smooth.

An anhinga ▶ stretches out its wings to dry them and absorb warmth from the sun. Its wing and tail feathers can be seen clearly.

▲ These pheasant feathers show how the contour feathers overlap each other.

A group of adult and ◀ five-month-old emperor penguins. The chicks have only soft down feathers.

They are held together by many tiny hooks that fasten on to each other. In most birds the contour feathers are arranged in regular rows on the bird's body. They overlap each other so that none of the skin is left uncovered.

The down feathers mostly lie underneath the contour feathers, next to the bird's skin. Down feathers are soft and fluffy. They help to keep the bird warm. Very young birds have only down feathers. Their contour feathers don't grow until later.

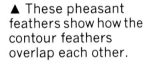

Contour feathers are held together by tiny hooks. The drawing in the circle shows a close-up of some of these hooks. Down feathers don't have hooks and are soft and fluffy.

FEATHER CARE

A bird's feathers need a lot of looking after. They must be kept in good condition because they are so important to the bird.

Birds use the edges of their beaks to smooth their feathers. This is called **preening**. They do this to get rid of dirt and to make sure that all the tiny hooks are properly joined together.

Most birds cover their feathers with oil to keep them supple and waterproof. They get the oil from the **preen gland** near their tails. A bird will cover its head and beak with oil from its preen gland. It will then spread the oil over the rest of its feathers.

This heron is preening. It will get rid of some of the dirt on its feathers by pulling them through its beak. It is important for birds to keep their feathers clean and tidy.

Did you know?

Some swans have more than 25,000 feathers. Some hummingbirds have fewer than 1000.

Some birds, such as herons and egrets, don't have preen glands. Instead they have feathers called **powder down** on their breasts. These feathers grow all the time. The tips break down into a fine waterproof powder that the bird can spread over its other feathers.

If a bird loses a feather it will grow a new one. All birds lose and replace all of their feathers regularly. This is called **molting**. Most small birds take three or four months to shed all their old feathers and grow new ones. Very large birds, such as eagles, may take longer.

Water drops roll off a goose's well-waterproofed feathers. ▲

This young albatross has started to molt. Its downy feathers will be replaced by adult plumage.

FEATHERS FOR DISPLAY

Many birds have very colorful feathers. Others appear very dull. Often the males of a particular kind of bird will be bright and showy and the females will be drab. Why should this be?

In many cases the males are brightly colored in order to attract a **mate**. The males with the brightest or most spectacular plumage are most attractive to the females.

The females, however, must not stand out while they are on the nest. If they did, they might draw the attention of a hunting animal and be eaten. Their feathers help to **camouflage** them by making them difficult to see against the background. The feathers of young birds also help them to stay hidden from hunters.

This male bird of paradise has a spectacular plumage. He will display his colors to attract a mate.

Often a bird's plumage is used to send a message to other birds of the same kind. The males of some kinds of birds will defend a patch of ground that they decide belongs to them. This is their **territory**. Males use their colorful feathers to display to each other in contests over territories.

A young bird's plumage doesn't only help to hide it. It is also telling its father that it is harmless and not a competing rival that should be chased off.

This wild turkey chick is well camouflaged among the dead leaves of the forest floor where it lives.

Both these birds are shining honeycreepers, but only the male is purple. The female's duller feathers will make her harder to see on the nest. ▼

THE ART OF FLYING

There are only a few birds that can't fly, such as ostriches and penguins. Almost all birds can fly. They are not the only animals that are able to fly – bats can fly, and, of course, so can many insects. How do they stay in the air?

Take a piece of paper and hold it loosely by the edge in front of you. Now blow hard across the *top* of the paper – not underneath it. Watch how the air flowing across the paper makes it rise up. It is air flowing over their wings that keeps birds and bats aloft. An airplane stays in the air in the same way.

Birds flapping their wings are not rowing themselves through the air. They move their wings forward to make the air flow over them. This lifts the bird up. A bird holds its wings at an angle to make sure that the flow of air across them will give it as much lift as possible.

This diagram shows ▶ a cross-section of the inner part of a bird's wing. Its curved shape means that air flows faster over the top than the bottom. This increases the lift.

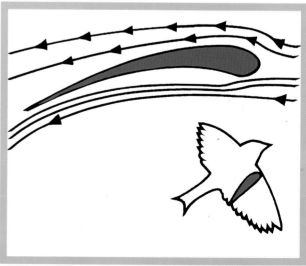

Did you know?

The wandering albatross has the biggest wingspan of all living birds – more than 11 feet. The biggest bird that ever flew had a wingspan of more than 23 feet. It is now extinct.

These pictures of a European robin show the flapping flight of a small bird.

◄ The wings of a hummingbird twist sharply as it hovers in one spot. The tips of the wings make a figure-eight pattern in the air.

The air doesn't simply lift the bird up, however; it also slows the bird down as it flies forward. This force that pulls the bird back is called **drag**. The wings of flying birds are shaped to cut smoothly through the air and keep down the drag.

Hummingbirds can hover in one spot like a helicopter. When they do this, there is no flow of air across their wings to keep them up. Instead, they lift themselves up by beating their wings very rapidly forward and backward. Their wings twist around so they are always pushing the bird up. By tilting its wings a hummingbird can fly one way or another. It can spin right around or even, just for a second or two, fly upside down!

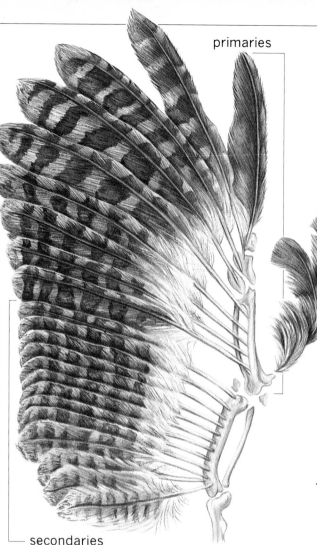

primaries

secondaries

BUILT TO FLY

There are several ways in which birds are built to fly. The most obvious, of course, is that instead of having front legs or arms and hands, birds have wings.

A bird's wing has two main sorts of feathers. The **primaries** are attached to the bones of what in other animals would be called the hand. They propel the bird through the air. It could not fly without its primaries.

The **secondaries** are attached to one of the bones of what would be the forearm in other animals. They provide a surface for the air to flow over and keep the bird up.

◄ This drawing shows how a bird's primary and secondary feathers are attached to its wing bones for extra strength.

Swans are among the heaviest flying birds. They have powerful chest muscles for strength, but still need a long, watery runway to build up enough speed to take off. ▼

The outer primary feathers and the inner secondary feathers are clearly seen on the wings of this white dove.

Flying requires a lot of strength, particularly taking off. When a bird takes off it has to provide all the lift by sheer muscle power until the air flow will support it.

Birds have large breast muscles to flap their wings. In some birds, such as pigeons, the breast muscles can make up a third of the bird's weight.

Weight is important in flying. The heavier a bird is the harder it will have to work in order to take off and fly. Birds have very light, hollow bones to cut down on weight. Some birds have skeletons that weigh only half as much as their feathers!

DIFFERENT WINGS

Birds have many different wing shapes. Even flightless birds have a use for their wings. The short and stubby wings of an ostrich help it to balance when it runs. Penguins have wings that are thin and flat, like paddles. They are very useful for swimming.

Warm air rises from the ground, or wind may be bounced upward from the side of a hill. Some birds with very broad wings, such as vultures, eagles and pelicans, can use the rising air to help them stay up. They glide effortlessly in this way for a long time. This kind of flying is called **soaring**.

Bubbles of air rise up ▶ from the ground when the ground is heated by the sun. Birds such as eagles ride on these bubbles so they don't have to use much energy flying.

An owl's wings feel like velvet. They are made in a way that allows the owl to fly silently so it will not be heard when it hunts.

Albatrosses are remarkable fliers. They can glide over the ocean waves for huge distances with scarcely a single flap of their long, narrow wings. They make use of the winds that blow over the ocean. Even if there is no wind, an albatross can still stay up by using the air that is pushed along by waves.

A gliding bird can change the amounts of lift and drag it gets by changing the shape of its wings. In this way it can speed up or slow down without flapping its wings.

Birds that live in woods and forests tend to have short, blunt-ended wings. This means that they cannot glide very easily. However, most of the time they are simply flying from tree to tree.

The long, narrow wings of the albatross are held straight out as it glides over the ocean with ease.

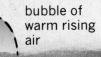

bubble of warm rising air

BEAKS

A bird has no arms and hands and must do everything with its feet and its beak. Almost all of the work of feeding is done with the beak.

Birds' beaks are not the same as the jaws of other animals. A bird's beak is in fact a horny covering on its jaw. A bird's jaw is much lighter than that of a reptile or mammal. A heavy head would make it more difficult for the bird to fly.

Because birds have no teeth, they cannot chew their food. Instead most have a **gizzard**. This is the part of a bird's digestive system where its food is ground up. The gizzard has very strong muscles to do this. Some birds swallow small stones. These are held in the gizzard, where they help to grind the food.

Birds don't only use their beaks for feeding. Some birds use beaks for fighting, courtship or display. Birds that build nests collect and carry nest-building materials in their beaks. Birds that live in burrows start digging the holes with their beaks but will use their feet to dig after that.

The beak of a toucan may be big, but it is not heavy. The toucan can skillfully use it to pick tiny berries. ▶

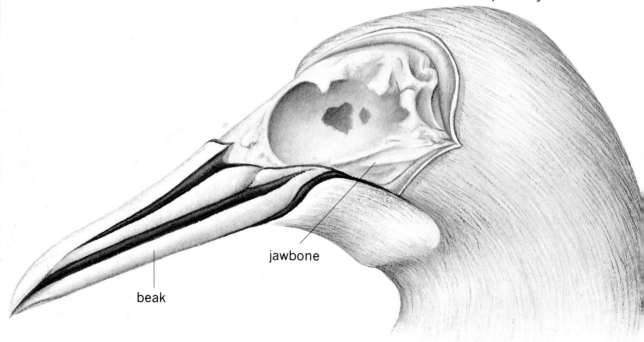

beak

jawbone

This is the skull of a gannet. It shows how the beak covers the bird's jaw.

Weaver birds use
only their beaks and
feet to make their
dangling nests of
woven grass. ▼

BEAK SHAPES

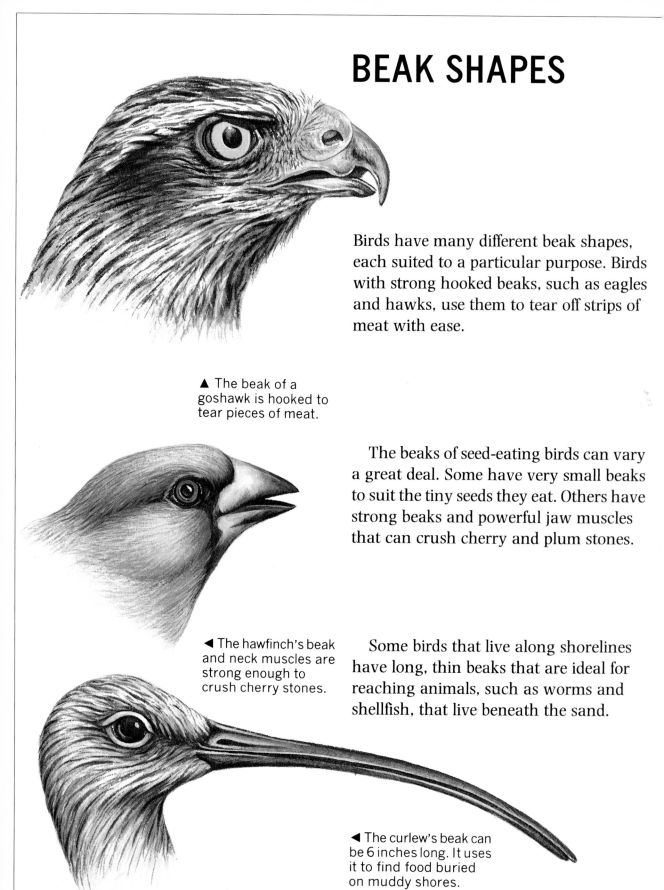

Birds have many different beak shapes, each suited to a particular purpose. Birds with strong hooked beaks, such as eagles and hawks, use them to tear off strips of meat with ease.

▲ The beak of a goshawk is hooked to tear pieces of meat.

The beaks of seed-eating birds can vary a great deal. Some have very small beaks to suit the tiny seeds they eat. Others have strong beaks and powerful jaw muscles that can crush cherry and plum stones.

◄ The hawfinch's beak and neck muscles are strong enough to crush cherry stones.

Some birds that live along shorelines have long, thin beaks that are ideal for reaching animals, such as worms and shellfish, that live beneath the sand.

◄ The curlew's beak can be 6 inches long. It uses it to find food buried on muddy shores.

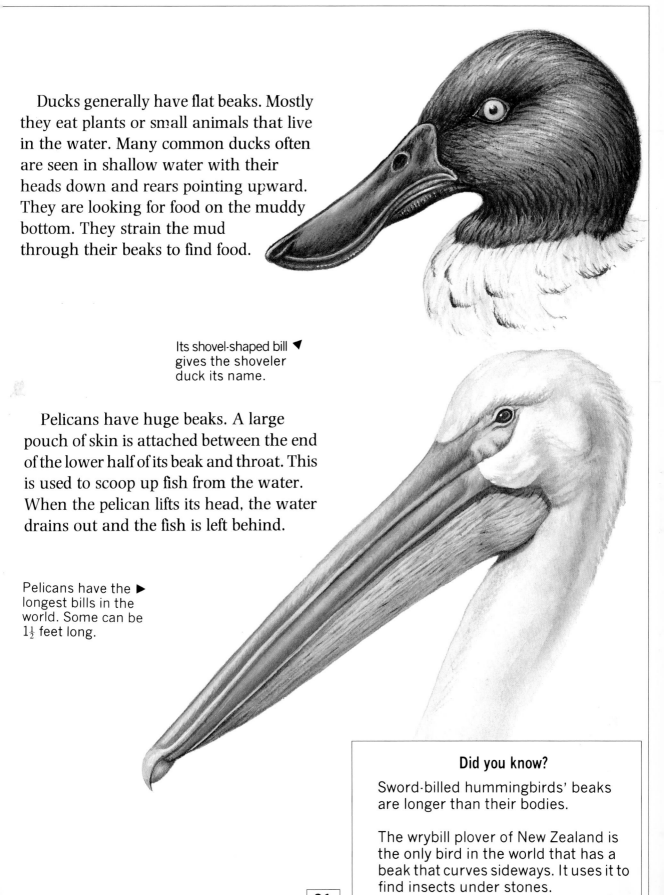

Ducks generally have flat beaks. Mostly they eat plants or small animals that live in the water. Many common ducks often are seen in shallow water with their heads down and rears pointing upward. They are looking for food on the muddy bottom. They strain the mud through their beaks to find food.

Its shovel-shaped bill ◀
gives the shoveler
duck its name.

Pelicans have huge beaks. A large pouch of skin is attached between the end of the lower half of its beak and throat. This is used to scoop up fish from the water. When the pelican lifts its head, the water drains out and the fish is left behind.

Pelicans have the ▶
longest bills in the
world. Some can be
$1\frac{1}{2}$ feet long.

Did you know?

Sword-billed hummingbirds' beaks are longer than their bodies.

The wrybill plover of New Zealand is the only bird in the world that has a beak that curves sideways. It uses it to find insects under stones.

21

SONGS AND CALLS

The reed warbler is able to sing two different songs at the same time.

Birds are not the only animals that sing. Male grasshoppers sing to attract females. Frogs sing to attract mates and defend their territories. Humans tend to do a lot of singing, too!

Frogs and humans have **vocal cords** near the top end of their throats that are made to vibrate to produce sounds. The voice box of a bird is at the bottom end of its throat. It is called the **syrinx**. Muscles around the syrinx can change its shape to make different sounds. Birds that do a lot of singing have complicated syrinxes. Some birds can even produce two different tunes at once and sing duets with themselves!

Not all birds have a syrinx. Some, such as vultures, are unable to sing, though they do make noises. Most birds, however, have a number of calls they use to send messages to one another. They might call to warn other birds of danger. Birds that fly together in flocks call to each other to keep the flock together.

Among the songbirds it is most often the male that sings. He is telling other birds of the same kind that this is where *he* lives – this is *his* territory. In spring, he may also be trying to attract a mate.

A whistling tree duck uses its whistlelike call to keep in touch with other birds in its flock when feeding in dense reed beds. ▼

The booming call of the bittern can be heard several miles away. ▶

EGG-LAYING

All female birds lay eggs. An egg provides food and protection for the growing young bird inside it. Birds are by no means the only living things to lay eggs. Insects and fish do, too. Most reptiles lay eggs, and even a few types of mammals do as well.

Why do birds lay eggs instead of having babies as humans do? One important reason is that it would be almost impossible for the female bird to fly if she had to carry her growing young inside her. Another advantage of eggs is that they can be left safely in a nest for a while if need be.

The number of eggs laid can vary enormously. Giant albatrosses lay only one egg every other year, for instance. European blackbirds, on the other hand, can often lay five eggs four times a year.

▲▲ This pheasant chick has to work hard to break out from its shell.

▲ A blackbird's nest showing a newly hatched chick.

◄ Chicks start off very small. The tiny red blob on the yolk of this egg will eventually become a chicken.

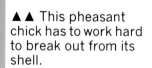

The shell of an egg contains **calcium**, among other things. Calcium is also found in bones. Female birds have a special kind of bone that they use to store calcium for their eggs. The shell of a hen's egg takes about fifteen hours to form inside the hen's body.

An eggshell has thousands of very tiny holes in it. These allow air to pass back and forth so that the growing chick inside can breathe.

Albatrosses lay only one egg every two years and so never have more than one chick at a time.

Inside the egg, as you will know if you have ever broken open a hen's egg, is the yellow **yolk** and the clear egg white, or **albumen**. The yolk is the growing bird's food supply. The albumen is like a cushion to protect the young bird. It is also a source of water.

EGG SHAPES

Birds' eggs come in a variety of different sizes, shapes and colors. The smallest eggs are, as you might expect, laid by the smallest birds. Some hummingbirds' eggs are less than a half-inch long and weigh less than 0.018 ounce. The eggs of the biggest bird, the ostrich, are huge. Ostrich eggs are about 7 inches long and can weigh about $4\frac{1}{2}$ pounds. This is almost forty times the weight of an average hen's egg.

The shape and color of a bird's eggs often tell you something about the way the bird lives. Birds that nest in holes or burrows have round eggs. These are white to show up better in the dark. Birds

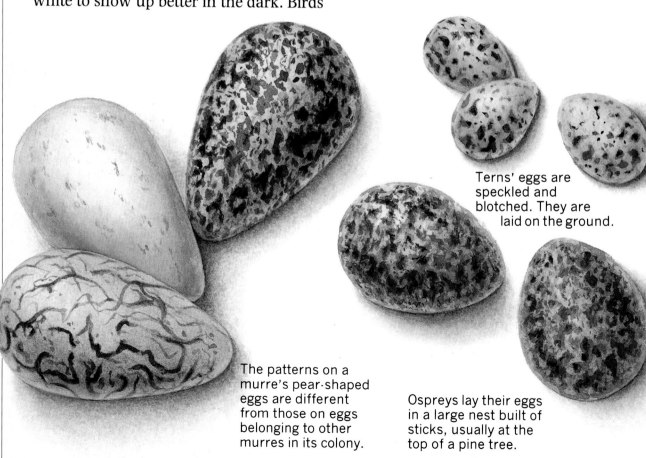

Lapwings lay their eggs in a nest on the ground. Their color helps to hide them.

The bright blue color of the dunnock's eggs make them easy to see if the female bird leaves the nest.

Hummingbirds have the smallest eggs of any type of bird.

Terns' eggs are speckled and blotched. They are laid on the ground.

The patterns on a murre's pear-shaped eggs are different from those on eggs belonging to other murres in its colony.

Ospreys lay their eggs in a large nest built of sticks, usually at the top of a pine tree.

A tawny owl's eggs are white so that the owl can see them in its dark nest.

that nest out in the open have eggs that are camouflaged. They are colored to blend in with the background. This helps the bird to hide them from animals that might want to eat them.

Some birds live together in large groups called **colonies**. When the parent bird returns to the colony after being away to feed, it has to find its own egg. Every egg has a different pattern to help the bird recognize its own.

One type of bird that lives in a colony is the murre. Murres lay their eggs on narrow cliff ledges high above the sea. Their eggs are pointed at one end like a pear. This means that if they are accidentally knocked they will spin around in a circle and not roll straight off the ledge and into the sea.

Murres live in large colonies on the edges of cliffs. Their eggs are specially shaped to stop them from rolling into the sea.

A WORLD OF BIRDS

There are almost 9000 different kinds of bird. They can be found living almost everywhere, in our towns and cities, in the tropical rain forests and in the frozen lands and icy seas around the poles. They range in size from the flightless ostrich, weighing 330 pounds and standing more than 8 feet tall, to the tiny bee hummingbird, weighing about 0.06 ounce and measuring less than $2\frac{1}{2}$ inches long.

Geese tend to fly in family groups. They are usually led by the older, more powerful female birds.

All birds, whatever their size or wherever they live, have certain things in common. They all have beaks. They all have wings, though not all birds can fly. The females all lay eggs. Most importantly, they all have feathers. Their feathers make birds special because they are the only living creatures that have them. All these things have made birds among the most successful animals on Earth. There are birds everywhere.

GLOSSARY

Albumen: The white of an egg. The albumen is clear and colorless. It surrounds the yellow yolk and protects the growing chick inside the egg.

Calcium: A necessary part of living things. Calcium is found in eggshells, bones and teeth.

Camouflage: Colors or patterns on a bird (or other animal) that blend into its surroundings, making the bird difficult to see. This helps the bird to hide from other animals that might want to eat it.

Colony: A large group of animals of the same kind that live together.

Contour feathers: These give a bird its shape and color. They are smooth and flat. Specially shaped contour feathers make up a bird's wings.

Down feathers: Small, soft and fluffy feathers that cover a bird's body and keep it warm. Young birds in the nest have only down feathers. In adult birds, the down feathers lie underneath and between the contour feathers.

Drag: The force that slows a bird or other flying thing down as it flies through the air.

Gizzard: Part of a bird's digestive system that breaks up food, as a bird has no teeth to do this job. It is strong and muscular and often contains small stones. The stones help to break the food up when the gizzard squeezes it.

Keratin: A strong but flexible material that is found in feathers, hair, horns and scales.

Mate: One of a pair of birds, or other animals, who together will raise young. One is male, the other female.

Molting: The process by which birds lose their old feathers and grow new ones. Molting usually takes either a few weeks or a few months, depending on the type of bird. A few of the larger kinds of bird, such as eagles, can take longer.

Plumage: All the feathers of a bird. Each kind of bird has a different shape and color plumage from other kinds of bird.

Powder down: Feathers a bit like down feathers that grow on the breasts of some birds, such as herons, that do not have preen glands. The tips of the powder down break up into a fine powder, like talcum, that the bird spreads over its other feathers. This helps to waterproof and clean them.

Preen gland: Part of a bird's body found near its tail. The preen gland produces oil that the bird uses to keep its feathers waterproof and in good condition.

Preening: What a bird does when it runs its feathers through its beak to clean and straighten them.

Primaries: The outermost feathers of a bird's wing. They are strong and flexible and propel the bird through the air.

Secondaries: The feathers of a bird's wing nearest its body. They form a curved "lifting" surface that keeps the bird in the air.

Soaring: Flying without flapping the wings. Birds that soar use natural air currents, such as warm rising air or the wind, to keep them up.

Syrinx: The part of a bird that makes the sound when it sings. The syrinx is found in the bird's throat. It vibrates to make sounds when air from the bird's lungs is passed over it. The syrinx is something like the vocal cords found in humans and some other animals. Not all kinds of birds have a syrinx.

Territory: An area that a bird or other animal lives in and will defend against others. Some birds sing to tell others where their territory is.

Vocal cords: The part of humans and other animals that produces the voice. The vocal cords are found in the throat. They vibrate to make sounds when air from the lungs is passed over them.

Yolk: The yellow part of an egg. It provides food for the growing chick inside the egg.

INDEX